PRAY
HEAR
WRITE

JEVON BOLDEN
Best-selling editor and writer

PRAY HEAR WRITE

21 DAYS OF PRAYER AND FASTING FOR BREAKTHROUGH IN YOUR WRITING

PRAY HEAR WRITE by Jevon Bolden
Published by Embolden Media Group
PO Box 953817
Lake Mary, FL 32795
www.emboldenmediagroup.com

This book or parts thereof may not be reproduced in any form, stored in a retrieval system, or transmitted in any form by any means—electronic, mechanical, photocopy, recording, or otherwise—without prior written permission of the publisher, except as provided by United States of America copyright law.

Unless otherwise noted, all Scripture quotations are taken from the New King James Version®. Copyright © 1982 by Thomas Nelson. Used by permission. All rights reserved.

Scripture quotations marked AMP are from the Amplified Bible. Copyright © 2015 by The Lockman Foundation, La Habra, CA 90631. All rights reserved. Used by permission.

Scripture quotations marked CEV are from the Contemporary English Version, copyright © 1995 by the American Bible Society. Used by permission.

Scripture quotations marked ESV are from the Holy Bible, English Standard Version. Copyright © 2001 by Crossway Bibles, a division of Good News Publishers. Used by permission.

Scripture quotations marked KJV are from the King James Version of the Bible.

Scripture quotations marked MEV are from the Modern English Version. Copyright © 2014 by Military Bible Association. Used by permission. All rights reserved.

Scripture quotations marked NIV are taken from the Holy Bible, New International Version®, NIV®. Copyright © 1973, 1978, 1984, 2011 by Biblica, Inc.™ Used by permission of Zondervan. All rights reserved worldwide. www.zondervan.com. The "NIV" and "New

International Version" are trademarks registered in the United States Patent and Trademark Office by Biblica, Inc.™

Scripture quotations marked NLT are from the Holy Bible, New Living Translation, copyright © 1996, 2004, 2007. Used by permission of Tyndale House Publishers, Inc., Wheaton, IL 60189. All rights reserved.

Scripture quotations marked THE MESSAGE are from *The Message: The Bible in Contemporary English*, copyright © 1993, 1994, 1995, 1996, 2000, 2001, 2002. Used by permission of NavPress Publishing Group.

Copyright © 2019 by Jevon Bolden
All rights reserved

Visit the author's website at www.jevonbolden.com.
International Standard Book Number:
978-0-9993544-5-2
E-book ISBN: 978-0-9993544-6-9

While the author has made every effort to provide accurate internet addresses at the time of publication, neither the publisher nor the author assumes any responsibility for errors or for changes that occur after publication. Further, the publisher does not have any control over and does not assume any responsibility for author or third-party websites or their content.

19 20 21 22 23 — 9 8 7 6 5 4 3 2 1
Printed in the United States of America

OH, THAT MY **WORDS** WERE WRITTEN.

OH! THAT THEY WERE INSCRIBED IN A **BOOK.**

—Job 19:23

CONTENTS

Introduction: It's Time to Pick Up Your Weapon..................1

Part 1: Setting Your Heart

1. Praying and Fasting for Your Writing......................................13
2. To What Fast Is He Calling You?..21
3. Prayer Focus: Set Your Expectations High..........................33

Part 2: Praying It Through

Day 1: The One Who Calls You Is Faithful..43
Day 2: You Have Heard Correctly..47
Day 3: You Are Part of a Great Company...51
Day 4: There's Room for You..55
Day 5: To Whom Are You Sent?..59
Day 6: In His Time...63
Day 7: A Wave of the Unseen and Unheard Of..............................67
Day 8: Contend for the Right Words...71
Day 9: Never Run Out of Good Things to Write...........................75
Day 10: The Well-Instructed Writer...79
Day 11: Like Fire Shut Up in Your Bones...83
Day 12: Inner Strength to Write...87
Day 13: Be Flexible...91
Day 14: Not Your Way but His..95
Day 15: Skilled and Gifted..99
Day 16: Tell Your Story Well..103
Day 17: Words of Life, Beacon of Light..107
Day 18: The Words of Your Testimony...111
Day 19: Shake Discouragement and Start with
What You Know..117

Day 20: An Expected End 123
Day 21: Do It for the "Well Done" 127

Part 3: Seeing It Manifest

4   What Did God Do? 135
5   It's Your Time to Shine! 141
     Appendix A: Confessions for the
     Spirit-Inspired Writer 155
     Appendix B: Inspired Book Ideas Log 159
     Appendix C: Divine Connections Tracker 201
     Notes 223
     About the Author 225

Introduction

IT'S TIME TO PICK UP YOUR WEAPON

For the weapons of our warfare are not carnal but mighty in God for pulling down strongholds.
—2 Corinthians 10:4

WRITER, YOU HAVE a unique weapon at your disposal that can bring healing to the world. That weapon is the written word. Just like any weapon, it can be wielded for good or evil. The right word at the right time can have a huge impact, if only on one reader at first, transforming them into a force of change and compassion and producing a ripple effect that can ultimately impact entire cultures and societies. Think about the literary or journalistic pieces some of the most influential people in history and in present times have read that caused them to be who they are.

Writers release healing words when they share their stories—fiction or nonfiction. When writers express their imaginations, share their convictions, or highlight the lives and stories of others through books, articles, blogs, or songs and poetry, they create fertile ground for understanding and empathy in the heart of the reader or listener.

Am I being too idealistic? Perhaps. But consider what happens to you when you pick up a book. Do you learn things you didn't know before? Do you feel emotions regarding the plight of the characters or subjects in the story? Do you travel in your mind to new geographic locations? Do you engage in the customs of cultures different from yours? Do you gain more knowledge about the author of the story? Do you learn about someone else's motivations or passions? Does your context of understanding people and the world around you expand? Does reading certain things cause you to know more about who you are? Are you challenged to be healthier, kinder, more positive, more confident, and so on? If you can answer yes to a few of these, then 1) I've proven my point, and 2) can you imagine how this could happen to readers of your works?

With what we see invading our online news feeds and shoving its way between our regularly scheduled television programming, we need more writers at this time writing with a goal to heal the infinite issues that we are facing.

Sometimes writers are criticized for not writing to trends and not saying what everybody else is saying in some type of unique or gimmicky way, and so they step outside of who they are just to get a byline or a publishing deal. And that's OK, if that's what God is requiring to cause doors to open for you. But please don't stop writing the words that heal the thing that keeps you up at night, the thing that brings tears to your eyes, the thing that makes you pound your fist on the table when discussing it with friends. Is it sex trafficking? Is it religious disunity? Is it race relations? Is it homelessness or poverty? Is it illiteracy? Is it gender bias in the church? Is it war, crime, or violence? Is it abuse? Is it people bound to cycles of poverty and failure?

You need to pick up your weapon and harness your power as a writer and begin to pull down the injustices, darkness, inequalities, and deceptions that keep so many from living their best life. It is time for you to wield your weapon and dismantle these enemies with the words you are being inspired to write.

Get a blog and write. Self-publish an e-book short. Then share the link with your two hundred Facebook friends, and maybe one will read your words and be changed or challenged forever. You never know who that one might be. It may even be you who's changed.

You're not new to writing. You've been writing all your life. Remember your first diary? You always had a love for words and a soft spot for hurting people. You have a power at your disposal that can be aligned with heaven to see change come for so many people and communities.

What you write breeds courage to start and finish difficult conversations. What you write challenges the status quo and rebels against harmful traditions. What you write tears down false ideologies. What you write builds bridges and closes the gap. What you write increases context and empathy. What you write illuminates what it is hidden in the dark. What you write restores brokenness. What you write unites what has been torn apart. What you write banishes fear. What you write renews hope. What you write sparks faith in the impossible. What you write inspires love. What you write heals. You know this, and you feel it.

Whether you need a fresh wind of strength and encouragement to keep at the writing you've already undertaken, whether you have put writing aside because of your own hurt or rejection and need healing and revival in that area, or whether you've just decided to answer the call that has long been poking at you, I believe that during these twenty-one days the fire and passion you need to fuel what God has commissioned and anointed you to do will burn hotter than ever.

There is a very real enemy who comes against all the good things God sets in motion, and you know him well. There are not many writing tips that say to simply pray and fast about your writing, but considering the level of attack that comes against writers and creatives of various kinds, all creative work should start right here.

Why Did I Write a Book Like This?

I am often asked how I am able to do all that I do, and I honestly have to say my first inclination is to answer, "All what?" All the editors and publishing professionals I know are so hardworking. They are some of the most generous people I know. I imagine there being so much more for me to do. I haven't hit the tip of the iceberg. Yet I can understand why I, among other working women, get questions like this. I ask the same questions of some of them myself.

Amidst being a business owner, wife, mom, student at times, and worship leader at others, God has blessed me with a wonderful career in books—all from sunny Florida and not the book publishing hub of New York City, though I have dreamed of living there. I can't take for granted the grace I've been given to develop some fantastic book ideas and concepts, author relationships, and strategies that have propelled the efforts of some of the teams I've been part of. He allowed me to pitch, write, and publish a major book in one week. Others have been pitched and published in longer duration times yet still with heroic levels of effort that only those behind the scenes may know. He has afforded me the grace to work with some of the most special people and to have edited and written more than four hundred books for children and adults in the last fifteen years, from Christian to mainstream, and from fiction to nonfiction with millions and millions of copies in print around the world. It's a blessing!

I never feel worthy or good enough to be the one chosen for such things, but I won't lie: I want to be chosen. So, when the opportunities arise, my yes is a no-brainer. I truly do think a lot like Tina Fey when she said, "Say yes, and you'll figure it out afterwards." Maya Angelou is also my inspiration here, when she said something in an interview with Oprah along the lines of, "I always say yes to good things."

Yes is the easy part, but then there's the actual thing.

It's not until after I've said yes that I remember how small I am. I write this chuckling because I know what I feel when I'm alone in my office with what I've said yes to. This is when I really need to tap into the strength and might of God. I begin the assignment, questioning why I said yes, how did I ever think I could get this done, and so on. You know the "this is absurd" routine. I am not alone here. I know that. So, for me, all my work—from mainstream to Christian, from personal to others-oriented—must be covered in prayer and, when it really gets big, fasting.

How do I do it? I'm nobody in this big world, but for those who've asked: I pray and fast.

I pray for a supernatural download from the Holy Spirit for strategies, ideas, and solutions on how to help my authors and writers like you write the best books possible that will influence the most lives as possible for the better. And what I have seen happen over and over again in my life and in the lives of those with whom I've partnered is that God answers. Innovation and ideas come—brilliant ones. Because of what it takes for me to get there, I can't ever take credit for any of the outcomes. It is truly that God is good all the time.

I write this book as an answer to how I do it and with the firm belief that prayer and fasting will work for you too as you say yes to God to write what He has called you to write.

Welcome to a New Season and a New Level of Writing

I'd like to invite you on a journey with me for the next twenty-one days to the throne room of God. I invite you to silence your mind, will, and intellect and let the Lord revive those desires He placed in your heart when He knew you before you were conceived in your mother's womb. Fasting brings a halt to the things in our natural selves that interrupt the supernatural. So, with prayer, I recommend that you fast as well. You have some dreams that you've been holding on to for a long time that need to materialize. You've been talking about it and holding out hope for it long enough. It's time to really let God in to do what He does best—finish and complete a work at which He can stand back and say, "That's good."

I've divided this book into three sections:

1. Setting Your Heart
2. Praying It Through—Twenty-One Days of Prayer, Fasting, and Devotion
3. Seeing It Manifest

These sections will help you to be very intentional about seeing your writing take the shape God's had in mind for it all along.

In "Setting Your Heart," I invite you to contemplate the attitude, focus, and expectations you will have as you set out on your fasting journey. I've included questions and spaces for listing your requests to God.

"Praying It Through" includes twenty-one days of prayers, devotions, and prayer prompts to help you pray God's will in your writing situation, to see breakthrough in your efforts of pulling together those right and forcible words that scatter darkness, and for the divine strategies needed so the right people get to read those words. I've also included journaling space for each day under the header "Pray. Hear. Write," so you can track in real-time what God is speaking to you.

I've made each of the journal pages about three pages long as a way of inviting you to adopt one of my favorite writing practices called morning pages—if only for these twenty-one days. Morning pages are just three pages written first thing in the morning about whatever is on your heart. This practice helps to break up any blockages to writing and creativity that may be in your way—and, in my experience, it will open you up to hearing God as you write and pray. To learn more about morning pages, check out my book *Break Through Writer's Block*.

Finally, "Seeing It Manifest" will serve as your place to record your proverbial "stones of remembrance," as found in Joshua 4. It is so very important to log what the Lord is saying and doing. Keeping a written record builds the great faith necessary to move the mountains that get in the way of you living out your scribal destiny and purpose. This is a section you can return to season after season to keep your expectancy high as God grows you from glory to glory.

I provided some additional resources at the end of the book in Appendixes A–C to give you more prayers and confessions to keep in front of you as you write as well as room to list and track the God-ideas for books and publishing connections you need to carry out your mission. Getting charged up just to write but not to release the word is just not good enough. I want to see you go all the way.

A special place in God's presence for the scribe

By God's grace, I've designed this book to be a Spirit-inspired writer's place to come before the Lord and soak in His presence specifically for their writing tasks. Scribes need this time—time when God is first and everything else is not, when it is His face only that we seek. It's in these times when we are seeking first the kingdom of God and His righteousness that everything else we may be praying about is added, including, "Lord, what do I write?" "You've called me, but what do I say?" "You've called me, but who is this word for?" "You've called me, but how will this word get out?"

As you humble yourself through fasting, I know God will come quickly to you with answers and inspiration from on high. You will be more passionate and driven than ever before to start and complete the work you've been commissioned by heaven to do. I know God will meet you. I pray that you will have countless revelatory moments during these twenty-one days and beyond. I pray that book titles and compelling hooks and summaries, chapter outlines, and arrow-sharp target audiences be downloaded to you.

Where you were stuck, I know you will be loosed. Where you were once rejected, you will be accepted according to God's plan. Where you were once discouraged and confused, you will be strengthened, encouraged, and clearly directed. He's done it for me so many times; I know He'll do it for you. I have no doubt.

Pray. Fast. Listen. Obey. Then pick up your weapon and write.

If you are ready for a breakthrough in your writing life, won't you join me these next twenty-one days as we boldly approach the throne of grace? You may just be a prayer away from the most significant writing experience of your life.

PART I

Setting your Heart

Set your heart and your soul to seek the Lord your God.
—1 Chronicles 22:19, kjv

1

PRAYING AND FASTING FOR YOUR WRITING

Pray without ceasing.
—1 Thessalonians 5:17

Men always ought to pray and not lose heart.
—Luke 18:1

This kind does not go out except by prayer and fasting.
—Matthew 17:21

P*RAY HEAR WRITE* is your pass to pray for yourself concerning your writing. You may be one to pray for others and go into spiritual warfare on their behalf, but you have a call too. Has it been lying dormant? What will you tell God when He comes back for receipts?

Whatever your stage in the writing continuum—veteran writer, aspiring, or new author—if you are writing on God's behalf, you must pray, and you must hear from Him. And there's so much that comes against being able to write, which I believe proves its worth and value.

Jesus said that we ought always to pray and never give up (Luke 18:1). He said that instead of getting anxious we should come to Him with thanksgiving and make our request known to Him about anything and everything through prayer (Phil. 4:6-7). Then He said that we have permission to approach His throne boldly with our concerns and that there we would find mercy and grace to help us in our "time of need" (Heb. 4:16).

I love that approaching God is not some hard and convoluted task. He says, "Come. What do you need? How can I help you accomplish what I put in your heart to do?" With this view of God's willingness to help, I encourage you to use this time to keep your writing projects lifted up before His throne. Take your concerns about timing and completion, marketing and publishing budget, audience and subject matter, your skill, and so on—take it all to the Lord. He knows the people, strategies, and skills you should employ to get the work done and get it done well.

As I've mentioned, I personally pray through each project I work on continuously—each word, each edit, each reader, and each author. I stay praying. I pray to know the mind and heart of God for each project. Truly, the books are God's things, holy and set apart. They are modern-day epistles of how the gospel continues to transform lives. How privileged am I to be able to put my hands on them!

I pray that as you embark on this prayer and fasting journey that you will cultivate a continuous attitude of prayer over all your writing assignments. As you inhale and exhale through each word you put on the page, pray that God's will be done. Put it in your mind to come to God first with every concern, insecurity, pressure, feeling of comparison, or financial need.

The books—or whatever you've been called to write—are His things. Like Hannah, you've prayed to bear them, but upon their birthing, dedicate them right back to

Him. Then do not forget to thank Him for your gift and the breakthroughs and success He brings to you as a result of that gift. He is so very gracious to count us worthy enough to carry such a high calling.

Open Your Heart to Receive the Word of the Lord

Many of the projects I am gifted at accomplishing are an uphill climb. Either I am faced with doctoring a book back to life due to some inadequacies on the part of the author, a schedule was truncated due to the necessity of the message getting to market at the right time, or any number of other issues. I know I am gifted to see through the complexity of each project and home in on what will make it clear, applicable, and easy to understand to the reading audience. I see it in my mind's eye, detangling it concept by concept and word by word. I wish I could explain it.

One of my favorite authors to work with, John Eckhardt, called it the can-opener anointing. Yeah. I am the Can Opener. He spoke these words to me in a meeting he was speaking at several years ago when he called my team and me to come up to the front for prayer:

> You will be the can opener that opens up the can. You will be the one that breaks open what is closed. You will be the one that's able to open up what others can't open up. For I am going to use you to open things up, saith the Lord, and to see what is hidden and to release it to the earth....that it may bring life, and nutrition, and health to the nations, says the Lord. So be My can opener and open up the can and release what has been hidden and locked to My people,

that they might eat and be blessed in the days to come.[1]

I'd always taken my work very seriously, but this word from the Lord showed me the divine reason why I was often assigned projects that others may not have been able to do. It allowed me to exchange any anxiety or stress I sometimes felt with grace, awareness, and purpose. I believe that the word of the Lord you receive during these twenty-one days will do for you what you need it to do so that you are thriving in grace and not striving in whatever it is that falsely fuels your actions.

Beginning Prayers to Prime Your Pump

It was about one month before I received this word of prophetic identity that I was working on a challenging project along the lines of what I mentioned above. I was struggling. It was hard. So I did what I knew to do: go into prayer-and-fasting mode. As I began to pray, I thought, "I bet there are others out there who may be struggling with projects of their own. Maybe as I pray I can share my prayers, and maybe they will help them too."

I originally posted the prayers on my blog,[2] but I believe they speak to what we're about to get into here. I pray these prayers believing…

1. God is on my side
2. He wouldn't have given me the assignment if He Himself didn't have faith in me
3. He has given me what I need to do the job well
4. He has a special reason for my being where I am at this particular time

I do this because I believe He wants me to tap into His infinite and divine resources to accomplish what is given to me. He said that He is with me and won't leave me (Matt. 28:20; Heb. 13:5). I think that His being with me shows His love, support, and awareness of where I am and what I need. I apply this understanding not only to my work but to everything in my life. Let these prayers strengthen and encourage you and cause you to perform better, create more, influence wider, and prosper greatly.

Prayers that release the writer's creative flow

> *I am creative and was made for this moment (Esther 4:14).*

> *I declare that as I am made in the image of God, I too have the ability to create something out of nothing (Gen. 1:26; Rom. 4:17). I declare that I will not fear the blank page. I will envision it full of inspiring and impactful words that will reach into the hearts of my readers (2 Tim. 1:7).*

> *I declare that I am focused and sharp (Isa. 26:3; 2 Tim. 1:7; Phil. 2:5).*

> *My concentration is impenetrable.*

> *I speak to all forces that seek to come against my creative thought processes to be still and dismissed from the atmosphere in the name of Jesus (Matt. 8:23–27).*

> *No spoken words, thoughts, curses, or dream-stealers (including my own) that*

have sought to destroy my gift will prosper in the name of Jesus (Isa. 54:17).

I have confidence in my God-given gifts as a writer and editor.

I am inspired by God.

Lord, grant me the supernatural ability in your Holy Spirit to hear what the Spirit is saying regarding the thing you would have me write or edit (Rev. 3:22).

Lord, I pray that as I write, these words will not come by the pure force of my will but that they flow out from Your Spirit (2 Pet. 1:21).

Grant me divine assurance to know when what I have written or edited is complete and pleasing to You (John 19:30).

God has given me every resource to do this work well. I declare that I will be a good steward of those resources and see the fruit of my labor prosper (Heb. 13:21; 2 Tim. 3:17; Matt. 25:14–30; Ps. 90:17). I release all anxiety and hypervigilance to "make this work," for it is not by my might or by my power that this work will reach its full potential, but it is by Your Spirit that this will be everything You are designing it to be (Zech. 4:6).

By His Spirit, You Will Write

Sometimes the things that try to get us off our game are things that cannot move by manpower or willpower.

We must invite the divine and supernatural in to give us power to get it done. The super-combination of prayer and fasting deals a deathblow to the enemy, enabling us to surpass all hindrances and soar to the heights of all God has in mind for us and our gifts.

> "Not by might nor by power, but by My Spirit," says the Lord of hosts. "Who are you, O great mountain? Before [me] you shall become a plain! And [I] shall bring forth [my writing in due season] with shouts of "Grace, grace to it!"
> —Zechariah 4:6–7

2

TO WHAT FAST IS HE CALLING YOU?

Is this not the fast that I have chosen?
—Isaiah 58:6

There are three aspects of this fast that will enhance your ability to write God's words.

1. Unusual Aptitude

Daniel spoke with the attendant who had been appointed by the chief of staff to look after Daniel, Hananiah, Mishael, and Azariah. "Please test us for ten days on a diet of vegetables and water….At the end of the ten days, see how we look compared to the other young men who are eating the king's food. Then make your decision in light of what you see." The attendant agreed to Daniel's suggestion and tested them for ten days.

At the end of the ten days, Daniel and his three friends looked healthier and better nourished than the young men who had been eating the food assigned by the king. So after that, the attendant fed them only vegetables instead of the food and wine provided for the others.

God gave these four young men *an unusual aptitude for understanding every aspect of literature and wisdom.* And God gave Daniel the special ability to interpret the meanings of visions and dreams.
—DANIEL 1:11–17, NLT, EMPHASIS ADDED

This passage has always been a point of strength for me and even a how-to. I've been passionate about literature and the power of the written word for as long as I've wondered about its place and mine in the body of Christ. We don't typically engage with literature in our churches except for that which directly relates to the Bible. What value did my aptitude for literature and developing book ideas add to the fivefold ministry? Which spiritual gift do *bibliophile* and *word nerd* fall under? And I love it all too, not just Christian books or topics. I've been a student of literature for most of my life.

In more recent years, I've come to understand my value to the kingdom of God, so I'm OK now. I also know I'm not alone. Many believers are widely read, but we need many more kingdom writers who understand both the literature of Babylon and the literature of heaven. We cannot afford to be on the outskirts trying to figure out how to be influential in this space. Our unusual aptitude in this area opens doors of power and influence that sit us at tables where the peace, joy, and goodness of the Holy Spirit can be released.

Daniel 1 confirms the value of a writer's education in a wide breadth of literature. In verse 4 (NLT) it says, "Train these young men in the language and literature of Babylon." These young men were not only reading Christian living and spiritual growth books, but it was all strategically placed in their academic curriculum to enhance their ability to bring glory to God through their gifts of "knowledge and good judgment" (v. 4, NLT). This is why I coach my authors and writers to read lots of books, and not just Christian ones.

One of the things I've found, having worked in both Christian and mainstream publishing, is that Christian writers do not read, and I am sad to report that our quality of writing and understanding of the book industry reflects that. Mainstream authors and writers read and are insatiable learners.

You must be open to God leading you to a strategy for growing and excelling in your gift of writing.

> Even so you, since you are zealous for spiritual gifts, let it be for the edification of the church that you seek to excel.
> —1 Corinthians 14:12

Don't be satisfied with good enough. Seek to be excellent. Look out for ways to receive that unusual aptitude. We often want God to do unusual things in our lives. Let's be ready to apply the unusual to what we offer back to Him.

Fasting opens your heart for not only supernatural ways of living in line with God's plan, but it also strengthens you to have discipline in the natural things as well. Think about how some may choose to fast to break certain habits, like eating sweets. Of course, the Lord can work in your heart to break the addiction, but then it is your responsibility to continue to practice staying away from sweets for the long-term and maybe replacing the craving with something that your body really needs.

Part of this fast is for you to pray that God will give

you *unusual* aptitude toward writing, first supernaturally, and then toward a practical yet better understanding of the mechanics of good writing, of styles and genres, of writing and conventions of literature. Then you can pray that He will give you the wisdom to know which is right for your book and how you can best execute it.

2. Spiritual Discernment and Clarity

> A message was revealed to Daniel….The message was true, but the appointed time was long; and he understood the message, and had understanding of the vision. In those days I, Daniel…ate no pleasant food, no meat or wine came into my mouth, nor did I anoint myself at all, till three whole weeks were fulfilled.
> —Daniel 10:1–3

Then Daniel fasted again when he was seeking the Lord for revelation concerning a matter that would affect the kingdom he served. You serve the kingdom of light. Your prayer and fasting during these three weeks or twenty-one days (however you wish to name the time frame) is for you to seek the Lord for His clear word concerning your call to write. Perhaps you've only heard so much, but you need more, such as timing or whom you should be writing to. Perhaps you need to be reminded of what was spoken. Whatever you need to know, God wants to tell you, and He meets with us in times when our spirits are humble, open, and focused.

> Call to Me, and I will answer you, and show you great and mighty things, which you do not know.
> —Jeremiah 33:3

> Surely the Lord God does nothing, unless He reveals His secret to His servants the prophets.
> —Amos 3:7

You are indeed prophetic as a writer who seeks to hear from God concerning what to write. The prophetic gift as described in the New Testament—different from the office of prophet within the fivefold ministry—is one that all believers have as we commune with God through prayer and worship. That we can know what God wants and can hear Him speak to us in the many ways He does identifies us as a prophetic people. This is the gift, available to us all, that you will be tapping into during your fast.

3. A Heart of Compassion Toward Your Readers

> Is this not the fast that I have chosen:
> To loose the bonds of wickedness,
> To undo the heavy burdens,
> To let the oppressed go free,
> And that you break every yoke?
> Is it not to share your bread with the hungry,
> And that you bring to your house the poor who
>   are cast out;
> When you see the naked, that you cover him,
> And not hide yourself from your own flesh?
> Then your light shall break forth like the morning,
> Your healing shall spring forth speedily,
> And your righteousness shall go before you;
> The glory of the Lord shall be your rear guard.
> Then you shall call, and the Lord will answer;
> You shall cry, and He will say, "Here I am."
> "If you take away the yoke from your midst,
> The pointing of the finger, and speaking
>   wickedness,

> If you extend your soul to the hungry
> And satisfy the afflicted soul,
> Then your light shall dawn in the darkness,
> And your darkness shall be as the noonday.
> The Lord will guide you continually,
> And satisfy your soul in drought,
> And strengthen your bones;
> You shall be like a watered garden,
> And like a spring of water, whose waters do not fail.
>
> —Isaiah 58:6–11

One of my core beliefs concerning writing is that it is a generous work. It is not about you or me; it is about your reader. Fasting to break your stubbornness to write only what you want to write with little consideration about how your message will reach your reader is what this aspect of fasting for breakthrough in your writing is about. It is absolutely this attitude you should desire: "Not my will but Thine be done."

Also called God's chosen fast, this fast is what prepares your heart to write God's word with the right balance, the right tone, and the right voice—writing the truth in love to those you've been called to set free, encourage, equip, empower, correct, entertain, heal, and so on.

You are writing truth that will set people free. While many write the truth, how is that truth conveyed? How does it need to be conveyed? Tone is the attitude with which you write. It can be "formal, informal, serious, comic, sarcastic, sad, or cheerful," and is conveyed through your choice of words."[1] Voice is your style as an author—"the quality that makes [your] writing unique, and which conveys [your] attitude, personality, and character."[2] These two literary devices shape your writing and have a significant impact on your message.

Sometimes it's necessary to be persuasive and

assertive in your writing because what you have to say must be taken seriously and the actions you put forth must be applied immediately. That's urgency.

Other times, you write the truth with compassion and gentleness as you nurse your readers back from grief, depression, loneliness, or failure. Will you write them out of their low place using a humorous voice? Will you teach them how to relaunch their ministry with a formal, instructive voice? Will you write to them as a partner in the faith or as an objective leader and authority? What you decide here is based on what your readers need. Going to God to request the right way to meet the needs of others is wise. He knows His children best. He may even lead you to an expert to help you arrive at the right answers.

This third part of the fast is for you to be moved with compassion, as Jesus was at the multitudes because they were like sheep without a shepherd. (See Matthew 9:36.) Sometimes He spoke assertively and strongly at people, stating facts and giving instruction. Other times He used humor and stories. Seek the Lord during these twenty-one days for the unique balance that authentically conveys your heart for the people to whom you've been called to write.

Bringing these three parts together, you will be able to set your heart toward God's perfect plan for how He desires your writing to advance the kingdom, bring you before great men and women, and preach the gospel to people from all walks of life.

How to Fast

In the Bible, fasting refers to fasting from food. However, in fasts longer than a few days, it is not recommended to fast entirely from food except for in extreme spiritual circumstances. This must absolutely be God-led and may need to include the counsel of your pastor and physician.

- Esther and Paul fasted three days from food and water. (See Esther 4:15–16; Acts 9:9.)
- Daniel and his friends initially fasted ten days from rich foods, dessert, delicacies, and meat. (See Daniel 1:12.) But then they carried out this diet for three years after proving that their dietary choices put them at an advantage over their peers.
- Daniel fasted again for twenty-one days from any pleasant food. (See Daniel 10:2–3.) We've taken this to mean that he essentially ate as some modern-day vegans do—no animal food products at all, only vegetables, fruit, whole grains, nuts, and legumes. Some versions of this fast exclude grains.
- Moses and Jesus fasted forty days with no food or water. This is a fast that is not recommended for the average person and certainly not for anyone with health issues. (See Exodus 24:18; 34:28; Luke 4:2.)

Then there are our more modern adaptations of fasting, which include:

- Fasting from sweets only
- Fasting from watching a favorite television program or the news

- Fasting from television watching altogether
- Fasting from social media
- Fasting one or two meals per day

   I will not tell you how you should fast. This is between you and the Lord. I will say that, as fasting has been part of my spiritual experience from a young age, I believe there is significance in the biblical fasting patterns with regard to both the duration and the purposes for which the individuals fasted. A twenty-one-day fast is just right when I need the word of the Lord over something I am doing or when I sense a need for heightened spiritual awareness.

   I have found that the most beneficial twenty-one-day fasts for me have included a strict whole food–only fast (no sugar or processed or packaged foods, with some meat) and/or a complete media fast, which included both social media and all of television. I've been "fasting" television for years now, actually. To jumpstart or end some of my fasting seasons, I have sometimes incorporated a three-day Esther fast.

   When it comes to developing written content, there is a stillness and quietness that needs to be cultivated that is really enhanced when there is no distraction from media. It allows me to get my mind off of what others are doing, my focus is unshakable, and I am able to get so much accomplished. When I fast from food, my own desires that arise from my flesh are subdued and submitted to the Spirit of God, and I can hear Him more clearly than at any other time.

When to Fast

The time to fast is another thing I believe is determined by the Spirit of God. When you can't hear the Lord or you need clarity that isn't readily coming, that may be a good time to fast. When you need physical or deep emotional healing, fasting may be good. When you need to strengthen your spiritual walk and devotion to God, fasting may be good.

Many people fast at the beginning of the year to set their goals and intentions for the year and to make sure they are God-led. I think a fast for your writing works well at the beginning of the year because it takes about twelve months to write, edit, promote, and publish a book. If you start writing and fasting in January, you could have the book completed by January the next year, which is the start of one of the best release seasons for new books.

Before you begin your twenty-one-day prayer journey, I recommend that you decide how you will fast and when. You may want to make up or search for a meal plan so that what you eat every day is not another kind of distraction. Then I suggest that you create a consistent devotional and writing time for yourself. You can also tag it on to your daily writing schedule. Each day of prayer prompts and devotions that I've written provide you some space to write. I know this will trigger an overflow of writing, so get ready. I'm so excited for what God will do for you over these next three weeks.

My *Pray Hear Write* Fasting Commitment

I, (your name) _____, commit to fasting and prayer for breakthrough in my writing. I desire to hear from God directly regarding the following areas:

- The concept(s) I am to write
- The words He desires me to write
- The genre, tone, and voice in which I should write
- The people to whom my writing will best benefit
- The strategy to get these words to them

My fast will begin on (enter the day and date): _____

and end on (enter the day and date): _____

For the next twenty-one days, I will fast from:

- _____
- _____
- _____

Every day, I commit to:

- Carry out my devotion and worship from _____ a.m./p.m. to _____ a.m./p.m.
- Set aside a dedicated writing time for _____ minutes/hours each day from _____ a.m./p.m. to _____.

During these times, I will:

1. Read the day's devotion included in this book.
2. Seek the Lord through focused prayer.
3. Wait on the Lord and hear His voice.
4. Write what He tells me.

I approach this fast:

- Believing that I am covered by the blood of Jesus, therefore I am righteous and welcomed in the presence of God where I can make my requests known to Him with thanksgiving in my heart.
- Humbly petitioning the throne of grace so that I may be empowered to initiate and complete the writing assignments God gives me.
- Believing that, when I ask for anything in the Jesus's name, He hears me, and if He hears me, I have what I am praying for.
- Believing that it is God's great delight to see the prosperity of His servants, that He withholds nothing good from me, and that He will give me the desires of my heart as I seek to glorify Him in the earth.

This is my solemn commitment, in Jesus's name.

Signed,

_____

(Your name)

3

PRAYER FOCUS—SET YOUR EXPECTATIONS HIGH

May the Lord answer your cry....May he send you help from his sanctuary and strengthen you from Jerusalem. May he remember all your gifts and look favorably on your burnt offerings. May he grant your heart's desires and make all your plans succeed. May we shout for joy when we hear of your victory and raise a victory banner in the name of our God. May the Lord answer all your prayers.

—Psalm 20:1–5, NLT

One of the things that touches my heart about Jesus's compassion for us is how He responds to our tentative and sometimes broken approach to Him concerning what we need. In Luke 5 there is the most precious exchange between Jesus and a man who had come to Him for healing. The passage reads:

> In one of the villages, Jesus met a man with an advanced case of leprosy. When the man saw Jesus, he bowed with his face to the ground,

> begging to be healed. "Lord," he said, "if you are willing, you can heal me and make me clean."
>
> Jesus reached out and touched him. "I am willing," he said. "Be healed!" And instantly the leprosy disappeared.
>
> —LUKE 5:12–13, NLT

Oh, my heart! Those three sweet words: "I am willing."

Whenever I am dealing with an onslaught of the enemy's darts of doubt, accusation, or guilt, I imagine my low and discouraged self coming to Him, as this man did. Approaching Jesus with a bowed face and begging, the leper did not seem to be confident that He was worthy to be in Jesus's presence and maybe not worthy of being healed either. He had been rejected, abandoned, isolated, and abused by family, friends, and townspeople. He had been left alone with his need. Whether your circumstances can realistically or figuratively compare, can you relate? God has blessed my life so much, yet I can relate. And still, reading this passage, my faith rises from whatever depths it may have momentarily dropped as I look up and envision Jesus saying to me, "I am willing."

As you come into these twenty-one days, bowed faced and maybe begging, what do you need Jesus to do for you? What troubles do you face seemingly alone that only He can heal? What are you desperate to see Him do in relation to your call and purpose to write and publish His words? Is it finances to support your dream? Is it the right connections? Is it breaking writers' block? Is it finding the right words or developing your idea into that sharp arrow the pierces the darkness? Is it getting healed in a certain place so that you may write as He's commanded? What do you need from Jesus in this season? Whatever it is, He is willing.

"Stretch Out Your Hand"

Jesus's command to the man with the withered hand in Matthew 12:10–13 to stretch out his hand was about this man's willingness to expose his limitation, frailty, and brokenness before Jesus. Would he be too embarrassed or proud to show his hand?

His obedience to Christ's request also revealed the level of faith and expectation he held concerning what this Man, Jesus, could do for him. We can look back on Jesus now and see His trail of miracles. We can see His undefeated record against the kingdom of darkness. But will we stretch out our hand?

I encourage you to use the list below to log what you hope to receive from God concerning your writing during these twenty-one days. I believe that making your requests known to God provides an opportunity to log His miracles and to praise Him for each one. Please, stretch out your hand.

Pray Hear Write

1.
2.
3.
4.
5.
6.
7.
8.
9.
10.

Prayer Focus—Set Your Expectations High

11.

12.

13.

14.

15.

16.

17.

18.

19.

20.

DO NOT NEGLECT YOUR *gift,* WHICH WAS GIVEN YOU THROUGH *prophecy* WHEN THE BODY OF ELDERS LAID THEIR HANDS ON YOU. BE DILIGENT IN THESE MATTERS; GIVE YOURSELF WHOLLY TO THEM, SO THAT EVERYONE MAY SEE YOUR *progress.*

—1 Timothy 4:14–15, NIV

PART II

Praying it Through

One thing I have desired of the Lord, that will I seek: that I may dwell in the house of the Lord all the days of my life, to behold the beauty of the Lord, and to inquire in His temple.

—Psalm 27:4

Day 1

THE ONE WHO CALLS YOU IS FAITHFUL

Looking unto Jesus the author and finisher of our faith; who for the joy that was set before him endured the cross, despising the shame, and is set down at the right hand of the throne of God.

—Hebrews 12:2, KJV

Being confident of this, that he who began a good work in you will carry it on to completion.

—Philippians 1:6, NIV

Writer,

Today, pray for your perseverance through the writing process. Pray that whatever the Lord has begun in you, He will bless you to see its completion. He is the faithful One who will do it through you. Do not grow weary. Do not faint. Keep writing. Stay diligent. Trust that in those weaker moments when you feel like you don't have much to give, a little goes a long way.

I pray that you will hold on to the promise that when you are faithful in the little things, He will make you ruler over much; that small, faithful beginnings make for strong finishes.

At points, it gets hard to see the gains you are making day by day, but there is a joy set before you. May you find strength in that joy.

May the Author and Finisher make Himself big in your writing process. May the promise you hold on to be that He who has begun a good work in you will be faithful to complete it.

Pray that God will release over you a finisher's anointing. Pray that you will have that extra power from on high to push through and complete what you've begun. May you be motivated by the joy that will be released in your heart upon seeing the finished product. Pray that you run your own race—looking neither to the left or to the right—and run it well. May you get the prize that comes with answering and being faithful to the high calling of God in Christ Jesus.

There really is nothing like finishing. You know that. So today, pray that you finish and finish well.

Pray. Hear. Write.

Praying It Through

Pray Hear Write

Day 2

YOU HAVE HEARD CORRECTLY

The Lord said to me, "You have seen correctly, for I am watching to see that my word is fulfilled."
—Jeremiah 1:12, NIV

WRITER,

Today pray that He will confirm that you have indeed seen and/or heard correctly as the word of the Lord has gone out both for your life and for the words you write for others . May He settle any second-guessing—"Did I hear that right?" "Is that really what You are showing me, God?" or "Am I to write this?"

"Yes," He says, "you have seen correctly. Yes, you have heard correctly. Now write it!"

Now I pray that He would watch over this same word, that it will perform the way He said it would. I rebuke any blockages, hindrances, and sabotages, in the name of Jesus. May the word of the Lord be fulfilled in your life and in your writing, in Jesus's name!

PRAY. HEAR. WRITE.

Praying It Through

Pray Hear Write

Day 3

YOU ARE PART OF A GREAT COMPANY

The Lord gave the word: great was the company of those that published it.
—Psalm 68:11, kjv

Writer,

I am pushing encouragement out to you today in this regard:

We, writers, are a great company. Don't ever feel alone in your assignment to write and publish the good news of Jesus. And then don't let the greatness (read *largeness* or *numerousness*) of the company make you feel that you aren't unique. This is a both/and situation. We are *both* a great company—a force—powerful, numerous, and hard to stop, *and* we each have significant and special parts to play in this whole work being accomplished.

Remember how Elijah was feeling isolated and alone in his fight to hold up the name of the Lord: "He said, I have been very zealous for the Lord God of hosts...and I, even I only, am left; and they seek my life, to take it away" (1 Kings 19:14, kjv). We feel like this sometimes.

We're alone in our writing corners, rooms, or studies with little to no support from family and friends. Sometimes spouses don't understand, and extra finances aren't there to invest. It can be very hard, but it gets better. Stick to it. Don't give up. There is a great company who knows the cost, who has remained faithful to the call despite difficulties. We're here with you.

Just as the angel of the Lord came to strengthen Elijah, to feed him, to lift him up from the pit of discouragement, and to say to him, "Yet I have left me seven thousand in Israel, all the knees which have not bowed unto Baal, and every mouth which hath not kissed him" (1 Kings 19:18, KJV), the Lord says to you now, "You are not alone. I will feed you and sustain you. There is a great company who also writes and publishes My words. Strengthen yourself and get back to work. 'Return on thy way' (v. 15, KJV)." And just as God gave Elijah step-by-step instructionson how to continue from where he was., He will do the same for you. Lean in to hear His instruction. He has given His word to you, and He will share with you His plan for how it is to be published. He will strengthen your heart for the work ahead.

Ask. Seek. Knock. Hear. Be strengthened. Be encouraged. Obey.

You are part of a great company of those who publish the word of the Lord.

Pray. Hear. Write.

_____

_____

_____

Praying It Through

Pray Hear Write

Day 4

THERE'S ROOM FOR YOU

*Do you see someone skilled in their work?
They will serve before kings; they will not
serve before officials of low rank.*

—Proverbs 22:29, niv

WRITER,

Pray that, as you are skilled in your writing work, God will cause you to serve before kings (CEOs, leaders, and people of great influence) and not before those of low rank. Pray that, even as you write the book now, He will begin making room for you. Pray that your writing gift makes room for you and brings you before great men (Prov. 18:16).

Let your gift be honored and respected.
Let it be in demand.
May you be sought out for your skill.
May you walk in favor because of your skill and gift.
May your skill increase more and more.
May you excel in your gift.
May doors be opened to you because of your gift—doors that only God opens and no man can shut.

May opportunity knock on your door because of your skill.

May you not lack one good thing because of your skill.

May your skill seat you at tables of influence and honor.

May your skill generate wealth and prosperity for you and your children.

May it go well with you as you utilize and excel in your gift and skill.

May you be accepted because you do well with your skill and gift.

May your skill point to the beauty and goodness of God.

May you walk humbly before the Lord, who has filled you with skill to do this work.

Pray. Hear. Write.

Praying It Through

Pray Hear Write

Day 5

TO WHOM ARE YOU SENT?

Son of man, take thee one stick, and write upon it, For Judah, and for the children of Israel his companions: then take another stick, and write upon it, For Joseph, the stick of Ephraim, and for all the house of Israel his companions.
—Ezekiel 37:16, KJV

Writer,

Today, pray and believe that God will show you just what to write and for whom you are to write. He will lead you to compelling book concepts and a specific target audience. God's word is like an arrow. It never misses.

Pray that God will sharpen your words and your focus and make them like arrows. Pray that He quickens your ears to hear what He is saying.

He says, "Call to Me, and I will answer you, and show you great and mighty things, which you do not know" (Jer. 33:3). What you don't know now about your writing, He will show you.

PRAY. HEAR. WRITE.

Praying It Through

PRAY HEAR WRITE

Day 6

IN HIS TIME

He has made everything beautiful in its time.
—Ecclesiastes 3:11

Writer,

You are not governed by man's profession of time. Today, pray that you will submit to the Lord's timing concerning your writing process, even while remaining vigilant to steward windows of opportunity and completing what you've started.

Too often we measure how much God is with us during the writing process based on how easy it is to write what we feel He's asked us to write. Sometimes writing is easy, and the words just flow. It's like you can't put the pen down, and you're staring at thirty thousand words out of seemingly nowhere. Other times, writing is hard, but that doesn't mean God isn't in it.

If writing is hard for you, don't be discouraged. Don't judge your progress by another writer's experience. Instead, keep your eyes on your own paper. Seek the Lord for confirmation that you are on the right track. Ask for an increase of discernment of the times and seasons operating in your writing life and be sensitive to His voice.

If writing came easy for you on one book, know that the next book could be different. The truth is, some books get written fast, and some books don't. Sometimes your most important messages take the longest to develop. Sometimes there's more that God wants you to see, experience, or know before He perfects His words in you.

Don't be hesitant to press into hard work and block off hours for writing when you need to. But also let God lead you through *your* process. Look forward to His making your words beautiful in His time.

Whether it's ten days, one year, or five years, He is faithful to complete the work He's begun in you.

Pray. Hear. Write.

_____

_____

_____

_____

_____

_____

_____

_____

_____

_____

Praying It Through

Pray Hear Write

Day 7

A WAVE OF THE UNSEEN AND UNHEARD OF

As it is written, Eye hath not seen, nor ear heard, neither have entered into the heart of man, the things which God hath prepared for them that love him.
—1 Corinthians 2:9, kjv

WRITER,

Over the years of working with writers and authors, I have at times gotten senses of what God is about to do. Recently I've been seeing that a wave is coming of something God is going to do through His people, especially writers and authors, in the days and months to come. I see a release of boldness to speak, preach, and write for those who may not have previously had it, for whatever reason; amplification of previously timid or silenced voices; a catapulting of those who've been hidden but have remained faithful and obedient.

Loving God is more than just words. He said, "If you love Me, keep My commandments" (John 14:15). In cross-referencing the concept of this verse with the Old Testament, we learn from the prophet Samuel that obedience is better than sacrifice (giving, offering; see

1 Sam. 15:22). God wants "clean hands and a pure heart" (Ps. 24:4). He wants the faithful (Luke 16:10).

For the faithful and obedient, there are things God has planned that no eye has seen and no ear has heard. To those who've been working faithfully behind the scenes, no eye has seen and no ear has heard what God has planned for you. Writers often put in years of working in isolation, and no one knows of their efforts until their work is released and their success breaks out. Often people see them as overnight successes. But we are learning the truth behind overnight success, even in this season. Over many nights of faithfulness, contending, and obedience do the successful see success. But when our light breaks through like the dawn (Isa. 58:8) and we are brought before great men (Prov. 18:16), people may think, "Wow, that was fast." But no. Through our love (obedience and faithfulness) for God, we have entered into the "no eye has seen, nor ear heard" realm. It was not overnight, but it was promised, and God always delivers on His promises and brings us to the *expected* end.

Today, pray that you are strengthened by the power of His might. Pray that you are refreshed by the promise that what God is preparing for you, no eye has seen and no ear has heard. Pray that you write and not grow weary, for in due season you will reap a great harvest (Gal. 6:9). Though you know what God is preparing for you will surely come, pray that His word manifests quickly.

What an exciting time for you to be alive. What a time for healing and restorative words to be released through you into the earth. Let God know how privileged you feel to be writing in times such as these. Pray that He be glorified in each stroke of your pen or keyboard, today and every day.

Pray. Hear. Write.

Pray Hear Write

Day 8

CONTEND FOR THE RIGHT WORDS

Can't you stick it out with me a single hour? Stay alert; be in prayer.
—Matthew 26:40, The Message

Writer,

Sometimes writing looks a lot like praying. Sometimes it looks a lot like contending. There is a word or message to be released onto that paper, but it needs spiritual force to bring it forth. It needs a humble and wholly submitted vessel to be released through. Sometimes we need to tarry, wait, watch, and stay alert in the presence of God until it comes. "Can we not stick it out with Him for even an hour?" Jesus asked.

Sometimes we give up too soon. Sometimes without full awareness we give in to the enemy telling us that writing is not for us: "You're not a writer. What could you have to write? Did you really hear God? The words would flow easier than this if He really wanted you to write."

Shut him up by staying right there in holy and submitted prayer. Just as you think to get up from your writing desk—to give up—the breaking point of revelation and surrender is right around the corner. Jesus said men ought to pray and never lose heart, never give up (Luke 18:1).

So it is from this place that I challenge you to pray today that you not want so much for that instant word, but you tarry and keep watch for the word in season, the mature word, the right and forcible word—God's word. That when the right word doesn't come the moment you sit down to write, you don't give up and think you've missed God, but you stay in His presence for even that hour as the Spirit leads. May you submit your will to His in that time. May His will be your will and His words your words. Not yours, but His be done.

Pray. Hear. Write.

_____

_____

_____

_____

_____

_____

_____

_____

_____

_____

_____

Praying It Through

Pray Hear Write

Day 9

NEVER RUN OUT OF GOOD THINGS TO WRITE

I'll write the book on your righteousness, talk up your salvation the livelong day, never run out of good things to write or say.

—Psalm 71:15, The Message

Writer,

As a believing writer, just about everything you write is a reflection of God's righteousness working in you. From fiction to nonfiction, to poetry and children's books, your words testify of the goodness, mercy, and salvation of the Lord. He made you righteous so that you would do amazing exploits for the kingdom.

Pray today for God to show you His righteousness weaved through the letters of your writing and the intentions of why you write, which is to ultimately see people healed, delivered, and set free. That can happen through any genre.

Pray today that, as you write, rivers of living water will flow out of you and onto the page. Let the springs of inspiration never dry up.

Pray that as you write the goodness of God

overwhelms you, that He restores to you the joy of your salvation, and that you never run out of good things to write.

Pray. Hear. Write.

_____
_____
_____
_____
_____
_____
_____
_____
_____
_____
_____
_____
_____
_____
_____
_____

Praying It Through

PRAY HEAR WRITE

Day 10

THE WELL-INSTRUCTED WRITER

The Sovereign Lord has given me a well-instructed tongue, to know the word that sustains the weary. He wakens me morning by morning, wakens my ear to listen like one being instructed.

—ISAIAH 50:4, NIV

WRITER,

Today, pray that, as you are awakened morning by morning with the awesome assignment to write, God will awaken your ears to listen as one who is being instructed. May you not write on a whim. May you not write without the weight of glory pressing upon your spirit. This is a high calling and an honor. You are so privileged. Pray that you value the moments where you can awaken to the voice of God instructing you word-by-word on what to write.

Pray that you are changed in those moments. If you were taking your writing in a wrong direction, pray for a heart that is open to God's instruction on how to get back on the right path. If you are writing with the wrong intentions, pray that the Lord purify your motives and instructs you on ways to write what He says to write. If you are writing with the wrong people in mind, may He instruct you on who His words are for.

You write His Words, and He blesses them and watches over them, that they will fulfill the purpose for which they were sent.

To be instructed by the Lord—what an enviable place to be! May you never leave that place.

Pray. Hear. Write.

_____
_____
_____
_____
_____
_____
_____
_____
_____
_____
_____
_____
_____

Praying It Through

PRAY HEAR WRITE

Day 11

LIKE FIRE SHUT UP IN YOUR BONES

If I say, "I will not mention his word or speak [or write] anymore in his name," his word is in my heart like a fire, a fire shut up in my bones. I am weary of holding it in; indeed, I cannot.

—JEREMIAH 20:9, NIV

WRITER,

Today is not the day to hold back the word of the Lord any longer. May His word be like fire shut up in your bones. May it burn until you become weary of holding it in. May you release it, saying, "Lord, I cannot hold it back anymore!"

Today, pray that the word of the Lord bubbles up in your spirit so strongly that you can barely hold your pen for writing so fast. May your fingers fly over the keyboard. May your dictation come forth like bullets. Let there be such a wave of urgency from the throne of heaven and such a demand on your writing that all you can do to calm it is to write as the Spirit gives you utterance, in Jesus's name.

May inspiration pour over you as you write.

PRAY. HEAR. WRITE.

Pray Hear Write

Day 12

INNER STRENGTH TO WRITE

I pray that from his glorious, unlimited resources [God] will empower you with inner strength through his Spirit.
—Ephesians 3:16, NLT

Writer,

Today, pray that God will empower you with inner strength from His Spirit to write and write well. Pray that He will give you:

Strength to finish what you've started

Strength to endure the process

Strength to say no to distractions

Strength to focus

Strength to pursue all He has for you through your writing

Strength to battle rejection, discouragement, and delays

Strength to overcome writer's block, financial block, or emotional or spiritual blocks

Strength to break through the residue of disappointment and past failure

Strength to believe you can do this

Strength to know you were chosen

Strength to act on the word of the Lord spoken over you

Strength to persist

Strength to believe it will be done as He said it would

Strength to get wealth and resources

Strength to discern what's beneficial and expedient now so that when the suddenlies come—and they will—you will be ready

In the name of Jesus, decree that mighty inner strength will be released in you today and the days to come as you obey the word of the Lord to write!

Pray. Hear. Write.

Praying It Through

Pray Hear Write

Day 13

BE FLEXIBLE

My dear friends, I really wanted to write you about God's saving power at work in our lives. But instead, I must write and ask you to defend the faith that God has once for all given to his people.
—Jude 1:3, CEV

Writer,

Today, pray for flexibility and agility in the Spirit when it comes to writing. The apostle Jude had planned to write a book about one thing, but the Lord led him in a different direction. Pray that you will be ready when the Lord wants to flip the script on you so that you can stay right in line with His right-now (*rhema*) word for His people.

Pray that by the power of God's Spirit you will remain tuned in to the subtle changes in the wind of the Spirit. When it blows left, you go left. When it blows right, you go right. Pray also that the Lord will download to you the strategy on how to shift the message or words. Would He have you repurpose what you began? Or do you put it aside for now and start fresh?

He is the Author and Finisher of your faith. Rely on

Him to lead you into all wisdom and into the way you should go with what He's commissioned you to write. Thank God for counting you a worthy servant with whom He shares these secrets.

Pray. Hear. Write.

_____
_____
_____
_____
_____
_____
_____
_____
_____
_____
_____
_____
_____
_____
_____
_____
_____
_____
_____
_____

Praying It Through

Pray Hear Write

Day 14

NOT YOUR WAY BUT HIS

Trust in the Lord with all your heart and lean not on your own understanding; in all your ways submit to him, and he will make your paths straight.
—PROVERBS 3:5–6, NIV

WRITER,
Pray that you refuse to fall to your natural, fleshly, human-made thought process and default solutions as you seek to complete the work of the Lord, writing your book.

Pray that God will make His presence big in your situations. Pray that you see no other way but His and that He keeps you on the straight and narrow path of His favor and blessing. His way is the way of life. It is full of wisdom, increase, and victory.

Declare to Him that while some trust in chariots and horses, you will trust in His name. His way. His strategy. Declare that you will not lean to your own understanding. What He has for you and your writing is better. You have a way of doing things, but He said, "My way is not your way." You have a way you think things should be accomplished, but He said, "My thoughts are higher than your thoughts." (See Isaiah 55:8–9.)

Pray to the Lord:

> *Bring me into the heavenly realm, O Lord, that I might sit in on and inquire of Your wisdom for this area of my life. Take the lead, O God, and I will follow. In Jesus's name, amen.*

Pray. Hear. Write.

Praying It Through

Pray Hear Write

Day 15

SKILLED AND GIFTED

He has filled them with skill to do all kinds of work.
—Exodus 35:35, NIV

Writer,

Writing is a skill that first comes from God. How we apply it and how we grow and excel in it is up to us.

I thank God for being the good Father He is—one who gives good gifts. He has filled you with the skill to write. Through your skill, people will be exposed to new levels of His glory and majesty. Today, pray that you will not only take your special endowment at its surface level but that you will seek to grow and excel in it.

The skilled artisans who built the sanctuary in Moses's time and the temple in Solomon's time were specifically chosen to lead out in that holy work because of their level of skill and craftsmanship. They were masters at what they did. Not just anything is good enough for God to inhabit, and you want the presence of God to dwell in your writing.

Writing is both a gift and a skill that can increase with use and training. Like craftsmen, you craft words of faith and hope. Like blacksmiths, you are a Spirit-led wordsmith.

Ask God to give you a revelation for this skill He's given you. Ask Him to teach you what it means to use it masterfully and help you to discern the times when He is saying to you, "Come up higher," "Increase here," and, "Level up there."

What you do is for Him, your God and King, that He may be glorified. You desire to please Him and to offer up a more excellent effort and expression as you serve Him with the gift He's entrusted to you. Invite Him into your heart to move it and enable you to bring His will to pass in your writing.

PRAY. HEAR. WRITE.

_____

_____

_____

_____

_____

_____

_____

_____

_____

_____

_____

Praying It Through

Pray Hear Write

Day 16

TELL YOUR STORY WELL

*Let the redeemed of the Lord tell their story—
those he redeemed from the hand of the
foe, those he gathered from the lands, from
east and west, from north and south.*
—Psalm 107:2–3, niv

Writer,

Today, pray for your confidence and boldness to tell your story and to tell it well. God has rescued and redeemed you from the hand of the enemy, and by you sharing your story, others will receive the faith and hope they need to see their redemption drawing near.

Pray that God would come in the midst of your writing this week. Ask Him to lay His hand upon your heart, mind, keyboard, and pen. Pray that He will give you supernatural grace to see yourself having written your story of His powerful hand invading your life and setting you free. Ask that He will give you the grace you need to empower you to write your story and to write it well.

Seek wisdom from the Lord today for how to do it. Write with conviction and humility. Write with the fervency and love of one who is reaching into the gates of hell, snatching out precious souls who would otherwise be burned (Jude 1:23). Thank God in advance for this grace. Thank Him for His permission and call to write. Declare that you have been redeemed from the hands of the enemy and that you will tell your story.

Pray. Hear. Write.

_____
_____
_____
_____
_____
_____
_____
_____
_____
_____
_____
_____
_____
_____

Praying It Through

Day 17

WORDS OF LIFE, BEACON OF LIGHT

You are seen as bright lights [beacons shining out clearly] in the world [of darkness], holding out and offering to everyone the word of life.

—Philippians 2:15–16, amp

Writer,

Today, pray and thank God for His words He downloads to you to bring light and life to those in dark places. You—Christian/Spirit-filled writer—ought to be prophetic in that you know how to tap into the Spirit of God through prayer, worship, Bible study, and fasting to hear what God is saying and then to write what you hear or see as He leads. The Bible says that His word is life. May you offer His word in your writing so that everyone who reads it may live.

Pray that, as you engage with your assignment to write, you get the refreshing sense that it is a light and beacon that illuminates the path that leads to God. May you be energized by the fact that His words that you write are life to those who read them. What an exciting and honorable opportunity!

May your words raise dead things back to the fullness of life in people who have long given up. May they raise to life hopes, dreams, relationships, sick bodies, finances, self-worth and self-esteem, and even trust in God. May your words be the forces through which their joy, fruitfulness, and peace are restored, their hearts are mended, their captivity is broken, their faith strengthened, and their bodies healed.

Let your heart overflow with praise to God for what an awesome thing it is that He has called you to. Truly, stand in awe.

Pray. Hear. Write.

Praying It Through

PRAY HEAR WRITE

Day 18

THE WORDS OF YOUR TESTIMONY

Now have come the salvation and the power and the kingdom of our God, and the authority of his Messiah. For the accuser of our brothers and sisters, who accuses them before our God day and night, has been hurled down.

They triumphed over him by the blood of the Lamb and by the word of their testimony; they did not love their lives so much as to shrink from death. Therefore rejoice, you heavens and you who dwell in them!

—Revelation 12:10–12, niv

Writer,

Today, pray for you and the power of your written story that will be released to the nations.

It is never for us to go about our work leaning upon our own wisdom and understanding, but one where we are able to depend on other gifts and resources to converge with ours to make our stories accomplish all that God would have them to do. In the past, many have written their stories from an isolated place with minimal exposure. That will not be our story. We have access to too much for us not to employ the information, technology, and resources God has laid at our fingertips. Look at what is at stake—souls!

We are competing for the minds and hearts of people amidst the noisiness and attractions of an enticing world. But through His Spirit, God has given various graces to the body of Christ so that we can come together, tap into heavenly wisdom, and push forward His gospel message and advance His kingdom. And at the very center of that is your testimony.

I am going to put a challenge out here to you. I challenge you to go beyond what you think is acceptable to you or what you think you know and reach out and see how God wants you to amplify Him and lift up His saving power in your life so the world may see it and be changed. (I can't help but see the image of you being that city on a hill from Matthew 5.)

Though we pray, there is also a time where prayer brings revelation and conviction for a change in mindset or direction, which then leads to action. God wants to do a new thing, and that is not always about the end game or the results. Sometimes that new thing starts with a new way of doing or seeing something.

What do you need to do differently today? In what areas do you see yourself needing a mind renewal regarding your approach to getting your story read and people set free and delivered? What part of your storytelling are you avoiding that you need to confront head on—you and God?

Would you pray this prayer with me?

> *Father, I pray that the limiting traps and accusations of the enemy be silenced that say I don't have what it takes or that my*

digging deeper into wisdom and strategy will be too hard or will slow my progress. I shut my ears to his lies. He has no authority over my life or my story, which have both been dedicated to You.

Lord, I acknowledge that this is Your work. You have called me to it, and I have submitted it to You. It is not mine to decide that I will just take control of it now that I have accepted Your call. Therefore, I submit to Your ways and Your thoughts toward it, which are higher than mine.

God, help me to see the big picture about what telling my story means to Your kingdom, what it means to potential readers, and the devastation it will have on death, hell, and the grave.

You said that I triumph over the enemy through my testimony and by the blood of the Lamb. God, make me bold to tell my story as big and loud as I can so all who hear it and read it will be blessed. I will not let the accuser continue to talk people out of salvation and all the blessings it brings.

May I write my testimony with love and prophetic vision. May I see my story impacting eternity. May my story populate heaven. In Jesus's name, amen.

Pray. Hear. Write.

Pray Hear Write

Praying It Through

PRAY HEAR WRITE

Day 19

SHAKE DISCOURAGEMENT AND START WITH WHAT YOU KNOW

In every thing give thanks: for this is the will of God in Christ Jesus concerning you.
—1 Thessalonians 5:18, kjv

Writer,

Delays, setbacks, tragedies, failures, disappointments, and other life challenges arise during the writing process. We are not sequestered to a safe zone while writing with someone else taking care of everything while we're away. Wouldn't that be dreamy?

In this and every season—the tough times too—we are approached with a fantastic invitation to look at all of life through a lens of thankfulness. In what way can we be grateful for the challenges and setbacks? In what way can we thank God for where we are right now, even if it doesn't look how we expected it to look?

We can start with what we know.

1. God Is with You

Psalm 23 has dug me out of some low places, and in verse 4 it says that even when we are walking through the valley of the shadow of death God is with us. He sends comfort and guidance. Have you ever broken down the phrase *valley of the shadow of death*? It sounds like the worst, most frightening, darkest place ever! Well, if you've ever been there, or anywhere in between, God was and is there too. That means a lot to me. We get a similar message from Hebrews 13:5: God will never leave us or forsake us. Knowing the character of God, that is an incredible promise for which we can shout, "Thank You, God! Thank You for being with me."

2. In All Things God Works

"And we know that *in all things* God works..." (Rom. 8:28, emphasis added). I'll stop there and let that preach for a second. God is working in all things concerning you, your life, and your writing. He is straightening paths, He is defending your honor, He is getting the right people in place, He is opening doors, He is bringing your name up in the minds of great people of influence, and more. He is working. This is all while it seems things just couldn't be going worse for some of us. *In all things God works*. Ask me how I know.

Delays, setbacks, and such are sometimes orchestrated to get you to the right place at the right time. Not too fast and not to slow, not ten degrees to the left, but right there, on the spot, and on time. Don't you love Him for that?

In these momentary afflictions that are common to us all, count it all joy and give thanks. You are one who loves God. You qualify for His working things out in your favor. Isn't that just so very good!

So today, pray and give God thanks in everything. It is His will for you to trust that He is working behind the scenes in ways you cannot yet fathom. Thank Him for what is working in your heart and character that is preparing you for His next level of favor. Get excited even in the not-so-good times because you know that in all things He is working. Hallelujah!

Put your foot down right now and declare that the devil will not steal your joy. He will not steal your praise. And he will not steal your fight to write with joy another day. You have a joy that is set before you that these challenges will not sabotage. You will stay focused in God's presence. You will keep your hand on the pen. If it's finances, writing—for now—doesn't cost a whole lot, so write until He releases what you need when you need it. Write until the appointed time comes to activate the strategies He's spoken to you in the secret place.

Thank God that, even in this, He is adding to the power of your testimony. Thank Him for what you are learning about Him and His ways and even about yourself, because it is adding more words to that book He told you to write.

Do not back down. Do not give up. Press forward, giving thanks to Him in all things. Let God know you love Him and that you honor His name and majesty. There is none like Him in all the earth.

Pray. Hear. Write.

_____

_____

_____

PRAY HEAR WRITE

Praying It Through

Pray Hear Write

Day 20

AN EXPECTED END

For I know the thoughts that I think toward you, saith the Lord, thoughts of peace, and not of evil, to give you an expected end.
—Jeremiah 29:11, kjv

Writer,

The phrase *expected end* stands out to me today. There are many translations and versions of Jeremiah 29:11 that give us phrases similar to "a future and a hope." And I absolutely love that. But the idea of expectation seems significant for today.

When God spoke this word to the people of Israel through the prophet Jeremiah, He was in the middle of telling them about their Babylonian captivity. I imagine that coming out of Egypt and hearing about the Promised Land and all the blessings, their expected end was not to be held captive again in another land. I imagine they left Egypt with a whole other end in mind.

What I like so much about this verse is that God is confirming that He will indeed bring them to their expected end of peace, prosperity, and blessing. It had not been forgotten or overlooked, but there was a process they had to travel through. Without going into all of the disbelief and rebellion that brought them where they were at the time of the events in this passage, I encourage you to pray today that your expected end will surely come.

Pray right now that the good intentions, the hopes, the excitement, the plans for book signings and successful book releases, the visions of changed lives and changed worlds be linked with God's thoughts toward you, that you might see that expected end.

You have expected success. You have expected to see yourself on the other side of completion. You have expected to see published books and articles, Bible studies and devotionals, and more. Pray now: "Lord, bring it to pass." As you are on this journey through rejection, waiting, doubts from others, doubts about ourselves, pray now: "Lord, let these things not hinder and keep me captive, but let me see my expected end. In Jesus's name, amen."

Pray. Hear. Write.

Praying It Through

Pray Hear Write

Day 21

DO IT FOR THE "WELL DONE"

> *His master said to him, "Well done, you good and faithful servant. You have been faithful over a few things. I will make you ruler over many things. Enter the joy of your master."*
>
> —Matthew 25:21, MEV

Writer,

Today, pray that you are being positioned to hear the Lord say, "Well done." Perhaps your writing gift has been stirred, and you've been writing a lot. Perhaps this has just been still and sacred time with very little writing. Whatever you've done, God is in the midst of you; you will not fail, especially not as you've poured your heart out to Him these twenty-one days.

Sometimes it gets hard to see our own progress amidst everyone else's, but we each have our own races to run, and every little bit gets us closer to the finish line. We each have a portion the Lord has given us to steward. How we invest in it and manage it according to His leading is where we get His "Well done."

If we miss the mark, we can make adjustments, forgive ourselves, and start again today. Even that—your strength to move forward despite setbacks—gets a "Well done."

Today, thank the Lord for the energy that is stirring up writers in this season. There is something powerful manifesting among God's people. Raise your expectations for the part God has destined you to play.

You may have invested thousands of prayers, thousands of words, and thousands of dollars into the writing dream God placed in you. It's good ground, and you will see a thousand-fold harvest if you don't lose heart.

Thank the Lord for the courage that is building in you and that you are bold enough to exhibit it as you reach out and ask and be taught. We don't know it all, but God has designated people and resources that will help us along each leg of the journey, and they will help us get a "Well done" at every turn. Pray that He shows you who they are and makes a way for you to work with them.

Thank God for the portion—the talent—He's entrusted to you. May you ever be faithful to steward and invest it well, so that you get the pleasure of hearing Him say, "Well done." Nothing in this life beats that.

Pray. Hear. Write.

_____

_____

_____

_____

_____

Praying It Through

PRAY HEAR WRITE

THUS SAYS THE LORD GOD OF

Israel,

"WRITE IN A BOOK ALL THE

words

WHICH I HAVE SPOKEN TO YOU."

—Jeremiah 30:2

PART III

Seeing It Manifest

Now this is the confidence that we have in Him, that if we ask anything according to His will, He hears us. And if we know that He hears us, whatever we ask, we know that we have the petitions that we have asked of Him.

—1 John 5:14–15

4

WHAT DID GOD DO?

And those twelve stones which they took out of the Jordan, Joshua set up in Gilgal. Then he spoke to the children of Israel, saying: "When your children ask their fathers in time to come, saying, 'What are these stones?' then you shall let your children know, saying, 'Israel crossed over this Jordan on dry land'; for the Lord your God dried up the waters of the Jordan before you until you had crossed over, as the Lord your God did to the Red Sea, which He dried up before us until we had crossed over, that all the peoples of the earth may know the hand of the Lord, that it is mighty, that you may fear the Lord your God forever."

—Joshua 4:20–24

There are three most important actions I believe we should take during times of strategic and focused prayer. They are:

1. Make our requests and petitions clear, which was done in the first part of this book.

2. Set our expectations high for what God will do, because He is willing to answer and He will do abundantly above all we ask or imagine. This is also what we made room in our hearts for at the beginning of this fast.
3. Being faithful to remember and record what God has done.

Like the twelve stones of remembrance the people of Israel placed by the Jordan, this page will serve as your memorial for all the things God has done for you during these twenty-one days. What you record here will give you faith and hope in seasons of writing when it feels like God is far away. These pages will help you press forward when everything around you is saying, "Give up," "You can't do this," or questioning, "Who will want to read your book?"

It is so important to remember what God has done. This page will contain the blessings, breakthrough, and deliverances you can raise as a standard against doubt, discouragement, fear, lack, or any other thing. Also, know that you are setting a legacy of great faith among your children—natural and spiritual—that God will do as He said and that He answers the prayers of the righteous.

So take some time now and look back. What has God done for you? How has He answered your prayers? What strategies, instructions, or words of encouragement has He given you? Write them out in the spaces below.

1. _____

_____

_____

What Did God Do?

2.

3.

4.

5.

6.

7.

8.

9.

10.

11.

12.

A Renewed Mind

Sometimes as we pray, the Holy Spirit renews our minds even in the way of what we think we need or want. Did that happen with you? Write about it here. What were the requests or needs you started with, and how were they adjusted, changed, or omitted along your twenty-one-day prayer journey? What did God do instead?

Pray Hear Write

5

IT'S YOUR TIME TO SHINE!
For Jesus, of Course

If I make you light-bearers, you don't think I'm going to hide you under a bucket, do you? I'm putting you on a light stand. Now that I've put you there on a hilltop, on a light stand—shine!

—Matthew 5:15, the Message

You have prayed and fasted and lifted your expectations into the heavenlies. It is time now to gaze down at Earth and reformulate your action plan based on what the Lord spoke to you over these twenty-one days. Fasting, for me, is a recharge and a way for me to hear God again on things I sometimes already knew. What is it like for you? What directives have you received?

_____

_____

_____

_____

Maybe you began your fast already clear of purpose and unshakable in your focus. Maybe you haven't even started your book. All you know is that God told you to write. So, prayerfully, as the assignment has been reconfirmed, revived, or clarified, I want to open you up to this challenge. Now that you know what you've been set in the earth to do is blessed and that you have all of heaven backing you, you have two jobs:

1. Write what God tells you to write.
2. Make sure it gets into the hands of people who need it most.

How? Platform. This is the six-letter *P*-word for many believing writers. Yes, you must build a platform. It's a cursed ask from book publishers and agents the world over. It also is a critical part of the puzzle for independent authors who want to see as many people as possible set free and delivered. Someone said something about this once that was a big wow for me: "How will they know who to invite if they don't know your name?" People must know you to get to the Jesus in you. The command to write is just one part of your mission.

The Fear of Building a Platform Is Common to Us All

If you are saying, "But I'm a Christian," as you read my words; if you have a sinking feeling in your heart that's saying, "This will never work. I'm supposed to be hidden. If I talk about my book too much, people will think I think it's all about me," then keep reading. You are not the only one who has felt this way, but there is too good a reason why you shouldn't.

This fear of being seen or making yourself known is a common thing I've noticed about new or aspiring Christian authors, especially women. I am not calling you out inappropriately, sisters. I've been doing this editing and acquisitions thing for almost two decades now, and women—Christian or not—are the most reluctant to let people know what they are doing. They are shy about showing their genuine excitement about their book and about sharing how it benefits their potential audience.

For believing authors, there is this fear of seeming self-centered, attention-seeking, and prideful as they increase their exposure and make their message of hope, love, peace, healing, deliverance, and abundance—i.e., salvation—available to more people. But increasing your exposure and making the good news of salvation available to more people is basically all your platform is.

Platform Is a Tool

In the old days, a platform was a box or some form of stage that a play actor or orator would stand on to be heard. They had something to say, some message to convey, but if they could not be seen, the message would not be heard. They would get lost in the hustle and bustle of the town. The platform was merely a means to amplify the voice of the speaker so they could be heard, much like a microphone.

Essentially, platform can be used to make anything louder—an idea, a message, a person. So platform is really a tool. It, in itself, is not self-serving or self-seeking, unless that is the user's goal.

We've sort of done with platform what we've done with money. Some of us have responded to wealth and abundance as if the verse says money is the root of all evil. (See 1 Timothy 6:10.) When it is clearly misplaced, inordinate affection toward money produces all sorts of evil. The Bible says money is the answer to everything (Eccles. 10:19) and it is a defense (Eccles. 7:12). While there's much to be revealed and unpacked concerning money, ultimately, money is a tool.

Platform is quite the same way. It is a tool to be used to amplify God's words spoken, written, sung, or demonstrated through us so that the world can see it, hear it, read it, and be blessed.

Platform Is Your City on a Hill

For believers, a few principles stand out to me, and they are encompassed in Matthew 5:13–16 in *The Message* version. It's one of my life verses.

> Let me tell you why you are here. You're here to be salt-seasoning that brings out the God-flavors

of this earth. If you lose your saltiness, how will people taste godliness? You've lost your usefulness and will end up in the garbage. Here's another way to put it: You're here to be light, bringing out the God-colors in the world. God is not a secret to be kept. We're going public with this, as public as a city on a hill. If I make you light-bearers, you don't think I'm going to hide you under a bucket, do you? I'm putting you on a light stand. Now that I've put you there on a hilltop, on a light stand—shine! Keep open house; be generous with your lives. By opening up to others, you'll prompt people to open up with God, this generous Father in heaven.

It is so exciting to me to live my life at home, at church, locally, nationally, and globally with the opportunity to show God's glory. I don't necessarily preach, but others do. I do what I do and answer yes to God at each level, hoping for the opportunity to lift His name higher. Some write, some heal, some speak, some counsel, some teach, some motivate, some deliver. Each of us has some gift or talent that is placed in us to amplify the glory of God in the earth. Why would we want to cover that up? And this is a serious question, because now we are talking about some issues of pride versus humility—and maybe even false humility. You know what I mean?

Where are our hearts? Why would we not answer yes to God? Why would we not inquire at His temple about how He has placed us in the world to be ambassadors and ministers of reconciliation? Why would we not stay at His throne and in His presence to remain both humble and confident that our gifts are making room for us and bringing us before great men? Why would we not want to find ways to draw people in and share our testimony, express the best methods we've experienced that cause heaven to come down to Earth, and tell how to cultivate the best and most miraculous atmospheres that bring healing and deliverance? Like, seriously we can draw as many people as possible through our unique callings and gifts.

Your Platform Lifts Up the Name of Jesus

When considering our platform, we must be careful that it be set up as an amplifier of the glory of God. All glory goes to Him. We are the rescued and humbled ones. We are the submitted ones. While our efforts all point to Him, everyone's platform will not look the same. We all have one, but some are big and broad. Others are targeted and specific.

Another principle is found in John 12:32: "And I, when I am lifted up from the earth, will draw all people to myself" (NIV). He empowers us by His Spirit to be His hands and feet in the earth. Filled with Christlike compassion toward the multitude who is without a shepherd, we should be moved in our hearts to offer what we have in service to God's plan and purpose for our lives. That includes rising and shining in the way He has designed us to. Again, it's hard to compare our shine to someone else's, but we each have one, and once we know what it is, we must steward it so that Jesus is always bigger and always praised.

> Arise, shine;
> For your light has come!
> And the glory of the LORD is risen upon you.
> For behold, the darkness shall cover the earth,
> And deep darkness the people;
> But the LORD will arise over you,
> And His glory will be seen upon you.

> The Gentiles shall come to your light,
> And kings to the brightness of your rising.
> Lift up your eyes all around, and see:
> They all gather together, they come to you.

This is from Isaiah 60. You should read and pray over the whole chapter. Let the Holy Spirit make this passage alive for you concerning platform building. It is so good.

Your Platform Propels Your Purpose

Platform is what comes with being human. We sort of just watch each other anyway. How we steward "the looking" is a whole other thing. Then as we are given our new life in God, He has a plan in mind for how He will love and bless us and return us to our original mandate, which is to be fruitful and to multiply, to fill the earth and to subdue it. To have dominion and authority. (See Genesis 1:28.) We do this as kingdom citizens now, pushing back the kingdom of darkness. His kingdom is in us, and as we increase, His kingdom increases. This seems like platform to me.

I'm in no place to discuss how people misuse platform, and, because of whatever weaknesses, take on too much of the glory for themselves and turn into other people and fall and bring shame to the name of God. That's a separate conversation. I mean, we are all so frail, but for the grace and mercy of God. Those negative results and missteps should not cloud our excitement for being ones who are charged with making the name of the Lord great. I mean, He is counting on us, right?

Your Platform Carries the Glory of God

A few of my authors call us believers "glory carriers." So while platform and spreading the glory of God to the ends of the earth isn't about you, it sort of is. You're an author who writes your salvation story in various forms, telling people about the Savior who rescued you. How will you get this message out? How will you carry the glory of God—boldly?

Don't be halfway with it, because you'll miss out on reaching the larger audience God wants His message to reach through you. You will keep doing half the assignment—writing the book—and not the other part, building the audience who'll read it. It's kind of like doing the "go" part of the Great Commission without making disciples.

Listen, there's not one thing wrong with being great at something—and don't let the devil make you ashamed for feeling greatness welling up in you. He loves to push us into false humility. Instead, educate yourself. Get knowledge, wisdom, and understanding. Build your platform so Jesus can be heard through you.

Ideas for How to Build Your Platform

You are walking into being both author and an entrepreneur, whether you self-publish or traditionally publish. Good business practices won't only build your success level; they will help you sustain success too. Building an audience of people who will read your work, attend your events, and share your content on social media is a wise business practice. How your audience responds—whether they do or don't—keeps you on your toes for providing great content that really makes the name of Jesus famous.

Platform and how it is measured are ever-changing. One part depends on how many social media followers you have, another part on how people actually engage with your message, and then how these numbers interact to create a ratio that shows publishers, agents, and yourself how your message resonates with your audience.

What I mean here is that it doesn't mean much if a person has twenty thousand followers but gets only one or two likes on each of their posts. That is a poor ratio that shows they have very little engagement and influence over their audience. It is likely that very few of their twenty thousand followers would click on the link let alone buy the book. But someone who has eight thousand followers and each post gets hundreds of likes and shares, they are showing signs of high engagement and an understanding of how to connect with their audience. If they were to post about a new book release, one could deduce that they would potentially sell hundreds maybe thousands of copies in no time.

So here are some ideas for how to grow a great community of engaged readers and increase the value of what you deliver to them.

1. Gather information and get knowledge about the book publishing industry and how other writers are doing well at building a platform.

- Several free and online resources are available. Start with a Google search. Follow an author or book publishing professional who offers resources and helps.
- Read books. One of note is *Platform* by Michael Hyatt.

- Consult with a book publishing/marketing professional.

2. Develop a plan that works for you.

- Consider how you will grow your platform. The following list includes just a few options that you can investigate—Google is your friend—and see what avenues work best for you. Then you can mix and match them in just the right order as you seek to bring your message to the masses.
- Social media
- Speaking engagements and other types of live or digital events, such as workshops, webinars, and book readings and signings
- Blogging and guest blogging.
- Podcast hosting or guesting
- Magazine writing—both in print and online
- Anthology writing
- Email and snail-mail lists

3. Be diligent and consistent in executing your plan.

Count the commitment as you begin to explore your various ideas. What time and effort can you consistently give to building your platform and adding value in the spaces in which you appear—digitally or in real life? Can you write one blog per week and post meaningful content to Facebook and Instagram three times a week? Or will one blog per month, daily posts to your preferred social network, and a weekly podcast be more your speed? Could you sprinkle in speaking at an event once per quarter and submitting an article idea to a magazine or other outlet two to three times a year?

Whatever combination you concoct, determine a frequency that works well for you, and build your plan into your daily schedule.

Look forward to being tenacious with your efforts. You must be diligent, and you must be consistent. Good content draws attention and generates the best marketing around—word of mouth. I consider even the shares in social media as a type of word-of-mouth promotion. The more people who share what you are saying, the more followers you attract and the more your influence grows.

Realize developing a strong platform rarely happens overnight. It is usually a slow, strong, and organic build, and the quality and engagement of people who are really sold out to what you have to say are worth the time and effort it takes to build them. They'll be loyal to you for life.

He Knows the Plans He Has for You!

I encourage you to take into prayer what I've shared about platform and about your time to shine after you feel the hand of the Lord leading you in that direction and once you've solidly understood what you are to write. Building a platform and writing a book often to go hand-in-hand, but it is a delicate balancing act making the moving parts of both tasks coexist harmoniously. Things can feel a little overwhelming and stressful, which is where the grace of God comes in. Remind yourself: It's not by your might or power, but it is by His Spirit that all will come together to build something unshakable.

I won't be surprised that, after bringing this book

along your writing journey and after you've finished writing your book, you decide you need to commit to another season of focused prayer, fasting, and listening to get God's input on how you should go about being salt and light (building a platform). When that time comes, I'll have some wonderful resources to support you in the quest.

Until then, I pray that this book has been a help to you and that you are able to hear God clearly concerning His plan to bring His gift of love, peace, and joy into the earth through the words you write. God plans to prosper you in your writing. All along the way, He plans to bless you exceedingly above all you could ask or imagine. He wants you to know what His plans are, and He will share them all with you as you ask, seek, and knock. Believe it, and do not doubt. Where He guides, He provides everything you need—nothing missing, nothing lacking, and nothing broken. Count on it.

"YES INDEED, IT WON'T BE LONG NOW"
God's Decree.
"THINGS ARE GOING TO HAPPEN SO FAST YOUR HEAD WILL SWIM, ONE THING FAST ON THE HEELS OF THE OTHER. YOU WON'T BE ABLE TO KEEP UP.
Everything
WILL BE HAPPENING AT ONCE—AND EVERYWHERE YOU LOOK,
blessings!
BLESSINGS LIKE WINE POURING OFF THE MOUNTAINS AND HILLS."

—Amos 9:13, The Message

Appendix A

CONFESSIONS FOR THE SPIRIT-INSPIRED WRITER

WRITER, YOU SPEAK, preach, teach, prophesy, inform, entertain, help, heal, strengthen, and encourage people through the words you write. Writing has the power of death and life. As a kingdom writer, you bring life and light to dead and dark places through the soul-saving words you write. Here are some declarations that will bring motivation, inspiration, and encouragement to you as you pour out your gift onto paper. God bless you as you write.

The Spirit of the Lord wrote by me, and His word was on my pen (2 Sam. 23:2).

The words I write uphold those who are stumbling. They strengthen feeble knees (Job 4:4).

I write words of life and light.

I write words of hope and expectation.

The words I write comfort others (1 Thess. 4:18)

I write the truth in love (Eph. 4:15).

I write what is upright. They are words of truth (Eccles. 12:10).

The words I write are pleasing and acceptable in the sight of the Lord (Ps. 19:14).

The words I write are forcible and right (Job 6:25).

I use beautiful words (Gen. 49:21).

I will not be dismayed. Words will not escape me (Job 32:15).

I write with knowledge, and my words have wisdom (Job 34:35).

The Lord gives ear to my words. He considers my written meditation (Ps. 5:1).

The word of the Lord comes to me.

Through my writing, the earth will hear the word of the Lord (Jer. 22:29).

As I write the words of the Lord, many will believe in Him (John 8:30).

The Holy Spirit will fall upon all those who read the words I write (Acts 10:44).

The words I write are wise like goads and scholarly like well-driven nails. They are given to me by the Shepherd (Eccles. 12:11).

I stand in the counsel of God and perceive and hear His word. I write what I hear (Jer. 23:18).

The word is near me. It is in my mouth and in my heart. It is the word of faith that I write (Rom. 10:8).

I consent to write wholesome words (1 Tim. 6:3).

I Write What God Says, Therefore...

The words I write are settled in heaven (Ps. 119:89).

The words I write are pure (Ps. 119:140).

The words I write are like silver tried in the furnace, purified seven times (Ps. 12:6).

The words I write grow and multiply (Acts 12:24).

The words I write grow mightily and prevail (Acts 19:20).

I Write, Therefore, Through My Writing...

I speak, and God speaks through me.

I send. I prophesy. I teach. I preach. I evangelize.

I heal. I deliver. I set free.

I edify. I encourage. I exhort.

I root out, pull down, destroy, throw down, build up, and plant.

I worship, and I praise.

I intercede, pray, and cry out.

I testify and overcome.

I bring joy, lift burdens, and strengthen.

I unify, and I divide.

I activate angels and stir up the miraculous.

I put God's glory and beauty on display.

Appendix B

INSPIRED BOOK IDEAS LOG

BY YOUR PRAYING and being in the presence of the Creator, you will rekindle the fire of your passion for writing and stir up the divine creative force that backs every good thing you do. Yes, God is going to give you book ideas during these twenty-one days. I know it. So here is a place for you to keep track of the best ideas He gives you during this time.

Though you don't need to fill in every line, trust that what He starts, He will finish. Don't be afraid to press in and pray through some of these ideas. Let Him bring them to their fullness. They may not all stick, but the ones that do—just you wait!

You'll need to hold on to this little book, and you may find yourself needing more than one for the various seasons you go through as a creative.

This appendix also offers you a place to create an outline for the books you will write and the beginnings of what's needed for a great book proposal. The many good things that God does all start with a good plan, counting the costs, and measuring resources. Here's a tool that will help you lay the foundation for much of your future Holy Spirit–inspired writings.

Book Idea #1

Book Title

Subtitle

Hook (a short, compelling statement that will apprehend the attention of your readers, an agent, or a publisher in 50 words or less)

Summary (250 words that tell what your book is about and how readers will benefit from reading it)

Inspired Book Ideas Log

_____

_____

_____

_____

_____

_____

_____

_____

_____

Target Audience (Names a specific type of person—the person to whom you are called, perhaps—who will be helped, encouraged, entertained, taught, or motivated from reading this book. "This book is for everyone" is not the answer to this one, as you know you are not called to minister to everyone. To whom is this book sent? "This book will appeal to readers who want to heal from the pain of their past and live in peace and freedom" is an example of a good start to defining of your target audience.)

_____

_____

_____

_____

Chapter Title and Topic Ideas

Introduction (Title):

_____

What's it about?

_____

_____

_____

_____

Chapter 2 (Title):

_____

What's it about?

_____

_____

_____

_____

Chapter 3 (Title):

_____

What's it about?

_____

_____

_____

_____

Chapter 4 (Title):

_____

What's it about?

_____

_____

_____

_____

Chapter 5 (Title):

_____

What's it about?

_____

_____

_____

_____

Chapter 6 (Title):

_____

What's it about?

_____

_____

_____

Chapter 7 (Title):

_____

What's it about?

_____

_____

_____

Chapter 8 (Title):

_____

What's it about?

_____

Inspired Book Ideas Log

Chapter 9 (Title):

What's it about?

Chapter 10 (Title):

What's it about?

Chapter 11 (Title):

What's it about?

Chapter 12 (Title):

What's it about?

Chapter 13 (Title):

What's it about?

Inspired Book Ideas Log

Chapter 14 (Title):

What's it about?

Chapter 15 (Title):

What's it about?

Book Idea #2

Book Title

Subtitle

Hook (a short, compelling statement that will apprehend the attention of your readers, an agent, or a publisher in 50 words or less)

Summary (250 words that tell what your book is about and how readers will benefit from reading it)

Inspired Book Ideas Log

_____
_____
_____
_____
_____
_____
_____
_____
_____

Target Audience (Names a specific type of person—the person to whom you are called, perhaps—who will be helped, encouraged, entertained, taught, or motivated from reading this book. "This book is for everyone" is not the answer to this one, as you know you are not called to minister to everyone. To whom is this book sent? "This book will appeal to readers who want to heal from the pain of their past and live in peace and freedom" is an example of a good start to defining of your target audience.)

_____
_____
_____
_____

Chapter Title and Topic Ideas

Introduction (Title):

_____

What's it about?

_____

_____

_____

_____

Chapter 2 (Title):

_____

What's it about?

_____

_____

_____

_____

Chapter 3 (Title):

_____

Inspired Book Ideas Log

What's it about?

___

___

___

___

Chapter 4 (Title):

___

What's it about?

___

___

___

___

Chapter 5 (Title):

___

What's it about?

___

___

___

___

Chapter 6 (Title):

What's it about?

Chapter 7 (Title):

What's it about?

Chapter 8 (Title):

What's it about?

Inspired Book Ideas Log

Chapter 9 (Title):

What's it about?

Chapter 10 (Title):

What's it about?

Chapter 11 (Title):

What's it about?

Chapter 12 (Title):

What's it about?

Chapter 13 (Title):

What's it about?

Chapter 14 (Title):

What's it about?

Chapter 15 (Title):

What's it about?

Book Idea #3

Book Title

Subtitle

Hook (a short, compelling statement that will apprehend the attention of your readers, an agent, or a publisher in 50 words or less)

Summary (250 words that tell what your book is about and how readers will benefit from reading it)

Inspired Book Ideas Log

_____

_____

_____

_____

_____

_____

_____

_____

_____

Target Audience (Names a specific type of person—the person to whom you are called, perhaps—who will be helped, encouraged, entertained, taught, or motivated from reading this book. "This book is for everyone" is not the answer to this one, as you know you are not called to minister to everyone. To whom is this book sent? "This book will appeal to readers who want to heal from the pain of their past and live in peace and freedom" is an example of a good start to defining of your target audience.)

_____

_____

_____

_____

Chapter Title and Topic Ideas

Introduction (Title):

_____

What's it about?

_____

_____

_____

_____

Chapter 2 (Title):

_____

What's it about?

_____

_____

_____

_____

Chapter 3 (Title):

_____

What's it about?

_____

_____

_____

_____

Chapter 4 (Title):

_____

What's it about?

_____

_____

_____

_____

Chapter 5 (Title):

_____

What's it about?

_____

_____

_____

_____

Chapter 6 (Title):

What's it about?

Chapter 7 (Title):

What's it about?

Chapter 8 (Title):

What's it about?

Inspired Book Ideas Log

Chapter 9 (Title):

What's it about?

Chapter 10 (Title):

What's it about?

Chapter 11 (Title):

_____

What's it about?

_____

_____

_____

Chapter 12 (Title):

_____

What's it about?

_____

_____

_____

Chapter 13 (Title):

_____

What's it about?

_____

Chapter 14 (Title):

What's it about?

Chapter 15 (Title):

What's it about?

Book Idea #4

Book Title

Subtitle

Hook (a short, compelling statement that will apprehend the attention of your readers, an agent, or a publisher in 50 words or less)

Summary (250 words that tell what your book is about and how readers will benefit from reading it)

Inspired Book Ideas Log

Target Audience (Names a specific type of person—the person to whom you are called, perhaps—who will be helped, encouraged, entertained, taught, or motivated from reading this book. "This book is for everyone" is not the answer to this one, as you know you are not called to minister to everyone. To whom is this book sent? "This book will appeal to readers who want to heal from the pain of their past and live in peace and freedom" is an example of a good start to defining of your target audience.)

Chapter Title and Topic Ideas

Introduction (Title):

What's it about?

Chapter 2 (Title):

What's it about?

Chapter 3 (Title):

What's it about?

Chapter 4 (Title):

What's it about?

Chapter 5 (Title):

What's it about?

Chapter 6 (Title):

What's it about?

Chapter 7 (Title):

What's it about?

Chapter 8 (Title):

What's it about?

Inspired Book Ideas Log

Chapter 9 (Title):

What's it about?

Chapter 10 (Title):

What's it about?

Chapter 11 (Title):

What's it about?

Chapter 12 (Title):

What's it about?

Chapter 13 (Title):

What's it about?

Inspired Book Ideas Log

Chapter 14 (Title):

What's it about?

Chapter 15 (Title):

What's it about?

Book Idea #5

Book Title

Subtitle

Hook (a short, compelling statement that will apprehend the attention of your readers, an agent, or a publisher in 50 words or less)

Summary (250 words that tell what your book is about and how readers will benefit from reading it)

Inspired Book Ideas Log

_____
_____
_____
_____
_____
_____
_____
_____
_____

Target Audience (Names a specific type of person—the person to whom you are called, perhaps—who will be helped, encouraged, entertained, taught, or motivated from reading this book. "This book is for everyone" is not the answer to this one, as you know you are not called to minister to everyone. To whom is this book sent? "This book will appeal to readers who want to heal from the pain of their past and live in peace and freedom" is an example of a good start to defining of your target audience.)

_____
_____
_____
_____

Chapter Title and Topic Ideas

Introduction (Title):

_____

What's it about?

_____

_____

_____

_____

Chapter 2 (Title):

_____

What's it about?

_____

_____

_____

_____

Chapter 3 (Title):

_____

What's it about?

_____

_____

_____

_____

Chapter 4 (Title):

_____

What's it about?

_____

_____

_____

_____

Chapter 5 (Title):

_____

What's it about?

_____

_____

_____

_____

Chapter 6 (Title):

What's it about?

Chapter 7 (Title):

What's it about?

Chapter 8 (Title):

What's it about?

Inspired Book Ideas Log

Chapter 9 (Title):

What's it about?

Chapter 10 (Title):

What's it about?

Chapter 11 (Title):

What's it about?

Chapter 12 (Title):

What's it about?

Chapter 13 (Title):

What's it about?

Inspired Book Ideas Log

Chapter 14 (Title):

What's it about?

Chapter 15 (Title):

What's it about?

Appendix C

DIVINE CONNECTIONS TRACKER

As you pray through these twenty-one days, God may lead you to the names of publishers, agents, editors, designers, marketing and promotions professionals, media outlets, ministries, or churches who would be like-minded potential partners with you to get your message into the lives of the people who need it. The names God leads you to may be the beginnings of your book publishing dream team. As you know, it takes a village to raise a book. Nobody truly does anything great on their own.

Here's a space for you to keep up with names and information for those whom God may prompt you to connect with. Use your answers for "What did God tell you about this contact?" to help form your introduction to that person or organization. What you tell them may cause something to leap in their spirit about what God may have been speaking to them in advance of your call or email.

Pray Hear Write

Contact #1

Date: _____

Type (circle one):   Publisher   Agent   Editor
                     Designer   Marketing
                     Media   Ministry
                     Other: _____

Name of contact: _____

Contact information

- Website: _____
- Email: _____
- Phone: _____

What did God tell you about this contact?

_____

_____

_____

What is your action step? What is He telling you to do?

_____

_____

_____

_____

When will you do it?

___

Follow-up date:

___

What was the result?

Pray Hear Write

Contact #2

Date: _____

Type (circle one): Publisher   Agent   Editor
                    Designer   Marketing
                    Media   Ministry
                    Other: _____

Name of contact: _____

Contact information

- Website: _____
- Email: _____
- Phone: _____

What did God tell you about this contact?

_____

_____

_____

What is your action step? What is He telling you to do?

_____

_____

_____

_____

_____

Divine Connections Tracker

When will you do it?

_____

_____

_____

Follow-up date:

_____

What was the result?

_____

_____

_____

_____

_____

_____

_____

_____

_____

_____

_____

_____

Contact #3

Date: _____

Type (circle one):   Publisher   Agent   Editor
                       Designer   Marketing
                       Media   Ministry
                       Other: _____

Name of contact: _____

Contact information

- Website: _____
- Email: _____
- Phone: _____

What did God tell you about this contact?

_____

_____

_____

What is your action step? What is He telling you to do?

_____

_____

_____

_____

_____

Divine Connections Tracker

When will you do it?

Follow-up date:

What was the result?

Contact #4

Date: _____

Type (circle one):   Publisher   Agent   Editor
                      Designer   Marketing
                      Media   Ministry
                      Other: _____

Name of contact: _____

Contact information

- Website: _____
- Email: _____
- Phone: _____

What did God tell you about this contact?

_____

_____

_____

What is your action step? What is He telling you to do?

_____

_____

_____

_____

_____

Divine Connections Tracker

When will you do it?

_____

_____

_____

Follow-up date:

_____

What was the result?

_____

_____

_____

_____

_____

_____

_____

_____

_____

_____

_____

_____

Contact #5

Date: _____

Type (circle one):   Publisher   Agent   Editor
                     Designer   Marketing
                     Media   Ministry
                     Other: _____

Name of contact: _____

Contact information

- Website: _____
- Email: _____
- Phone: _____

What did God tell you about this contact?

_____

_____

_____

What is your action step? What is He telling you to do?

_____

_____

_____

_____

_____

Divine Connections Tracker

When will you do it?

Follow-up date:

What was the result?

Contact #6

Date: _____

Type (circle one):   Publisher   Agent   Editor
                      Designer   Marketing
                      Media   Ministry
                      Other: _____

Name of contact: _____

Contact information

- Website: _____
- Email: _____
- Phone: _____

What did God tell you about this contact?

_____

_____

_____

What is your action step? What is He telling you to do?

_____

_____

_____

_____

_____

Divine Connections Tracker

When will you do it?

_____

_____

_____

Follow-up date:

_____

What was the result?

_____

_____

_____

_____

_____

_____

_____

_____

_____

_____

_____

_____

Contact #7

Date: _____

Type (circle one):   Publisher   Agent   Editor
                     Designer   Marketing
                     Media   Ministry
                     Other: _____

Name of contact: _____

Contact information

- Website: _____
- Email: _____
- Phone: _____

What did God tell you about this contact?

_____

_____

_____

What is your action step? What is He telling you to do?

_____

_____

_____

_____

_____

Divine Connections Tracker

When will you do it?

Follow-up date:

What was the result?

Pray Hear Write

Contact #8

Date: _____

Type (circle one):   Publisher   Agent   Editor
                      Designer   Marketing
                      Media   Ministry
                      Other: _____

Name of contact: _____

Contact information

- Website: _____
- Email: _____
- Phone: _____

What did God tell you about this contact?

_____

_____

_____

What is your action step? What is He telling you to do?

_____

_____

_____

_____

_____

When will you do it?

_____

_____

_____

Follow-up date:

_____

What was the result?

_____

_____

_____

_____

_____

_____

_____

_____

_____

_____

_____

_____

Contact #9

Date: _____

Type (circle one): Publisher   Agent   Editor
                    Designer   Marketing
                    Media   Ministry
                    Other: _____

Name of contact: _____

Contact information

- Website: _____
- Email: _____
- Phone: _____

What did God tell you about this contact?

_____

_____

_____

What is your action step? What is He telling you to do?

_____

_____

_____

_____

Divine Connections Tracker

When will you do it?

Follow-up date:

What was the result?

Contact #10

Date: _____

Type (circle one):   Publisher   Agent   Editor
                     Designer   Marketing
                     Media   Ministry
                     Other: _____

Name of contact: _____

Contact information

- Website: _____
- Email: _____
- Phone: _____

What did God tell you about this contact?

_____
_____
_____

What is your action step? What is He telling you to do?

_____
_____
_____
_____
_____

Divine Connections Tracker

When will you do it?

_____

_____

_____

Follow-up date:

_____

What was the result?

_____

_____

_____

_____

_____

_____

_____

_____

_____

_____

_____

NOTES

Chapter 1: Praying and Fasting for Your Writing

1. John Eckhardt, speaking at KDM Conference at Spoken Word Ministries, Jacksonville, FL, April 28, 2012. Used with permission.
2. Jevon Bolden, "Prayers That Release Writer and Editor Creative Flow," JevonBolden.com, March 29, 2012, https://www.jevonbolden.com/blog//2012/03/prayers-that-release-writer-and-editor.html.

Chapter 2: To What Fast Is He Calling You?

1. "Tone," LiteraryDevices.net, https://literarydevices.net/tone/.
2. Ginny Wiehardt, "Learn About Author's Voice in Fiction Writing," TheBalancedCareers.com, April 30, 2018, https://www.thebalancecareers.com/what-is-voice-in-fiction-writing-1277142.

ABOUT THE AUTHOR

JEVON BOLDEN IS a book editor, writer, literary agent, and CEO of Embolden Media Group, a boutique publishing consulting firm. She is best known for her work with Christian best-selling authors such as John Eckhardt, Michelle McClain-Walters, William McDowell, Don Colbert, and Cherie Calbom, a.k.a. "the Juice Lady."

She has served as senior editor for both Christian and mainstream publishers, acquiring and developing content on topics ranging from natural health and wellness to spiritual and personal growth, Christian living, and children's nonfiction. The books she has written as other people have appeared on ECPA and CBA best-seller lists and have sold hundreds of thousands of copies around the world.

As a conference speaker, workshop facilitator, writing coach, and mentor, Jevon shares the best of what she knows with passionate, creative, and influential individuals and groups around the country, inspiring them to publish great books that make a difference.

Jevon is married with two children and lives her best life helping authors change the world, one word at a time, from her home in sunny Florida.

Connect with her:
www.jevonbolden.com

 Jevon Bolden, Editor  @jevonbolden

 @jevonbolden   info@jevonbolden.com

CPSIA information can be obtained
at www.ICGtesting.com
Printed in the USA
BVHW011618040819
555042BV00008BA/97/P